The SUPER Book of Phonics Poems

by Linda B. Ross

88 Playful Poems With Easy Lessons That Teach Consonants, Vowels, Blends, Digraphs, and Much More!

SCHOLASTIC
PROFESSIONAL BOOKS

New York • Toronto • London • Auckland • Sydney
Mexico City • New Delhi • Hong Kong

Dedication

To my father, whose love and kindness added
poetry to my life and to the lives of others

Cover design by Norma Ortiz
Cover artwork by Anne Kennedy
Interior artwork by Patrick Girouard,
except pages 5 and 7 by James Graham Hale,
and page 6 by Abby Carter
Interior design by Grafica, Inc.

ISBN: 0-439-16032-4
Copyright © 2000 by Linda B. Ross
All rights reserved.
Printed in the U.S.A.

Contents

Contents

Introduction

No matter what method you use to teach your students to read—*The Super Book of Phonics Poems* can serve as a valuable resource that will enhance and energize the phonics instruction in your reading program.

Using poems and rhymes is an effective and natural way for children to build their phonemic awareness and phonics skills. The rhyme, rhythm, and repetition in poems provide natural and motivating models for teaching the sounds of our language. By using poems that appeal to children and make them smile, you can remove the label of "drill" from phonics and make it lively and interesting for your students.

How to Use This Book

Poems for Each Sound-Letter Relationship
In this section of the book, you will find one or two poems for each of the important sound-letter relationships that are taught in kindergarten through third grade. If you take a look at the Contents, you will see that the phonics skills have been organized into the following categories: consonants, short vowels, long vowels (vowel-consonant-e), more long vowel combinations, r-controlled vowels, variant vowels and diphthongs, consonant blends, and consonant digraphs. On the poetry pages, the phonics elements that are being emphasized are always shown in **bold** type.

While the poems target specific sound-letter relationships, they also deal with concepts and ideas that interest young children, such as the seasons, colors, animals, friends, and having fun. Some of the poems are silly, such as the one about two giraffes having a race; others deal with more serious topics, such as moving away or missing a friend. However, all of the poems have strong rhyme and rhythm patterns and were written to speak directly to children—to involve and delight them.

Teaching Strategies
In the section that begins below, you will find teaching strategies for presenting and using the phonics poems in your classroom. Following the strategies are a variety of interesting activities to help children practice and reinforce the sound-letter relationships that have been introduced through the poems. You will also find a model of a school-to-home letter that can be sent home with any poem. (See page 8.) The letter explains to parents and caregivers what sound-letter relationship has been taught and offers some general suggestions for using the poem at home.

Teaching Strategies

Introducing the Poem Before you read the poem, you may want to prepare children by giving them a brief description of what the poem is about and asking them to listen for the targeted sound. For example, for the poem "Rex and Rory," you might tell children that the poem is about two raccoons who go to the library, and encourage them to listen for the sound /r/.

If you are presenting the sound for the first time, you may want to read the poem without displaying it so that children can focus on the sound of the letter(s) before tackling the sound-symbol relationship. If you are reviewing the sound, you may want to write the poem on chart paper or on sentence strips to place in a pocket chart. You can highlight the targeted phonics element by writing the letter(s) in a second color.

Read the poem twice to enable children to listen to the sounds of the words as well as to understand the content of the poem. Then briefly discuss the poem and allow children to give their personal responses. For example, after reading "Rex and Rory," you might ask: *Did you like the poem? Why? Do you go to the library to listen to stories? What kinds of stories do you like to hear?* and so on.

Rereading the Poem During subsequent readings of the poem, ask children to perform a specific action each time they hear the targeted sound:

- Raise a hand each time they hear words with the targeted sound.

- Stand up, sit down, jump, or hop each time they hear words with the targeted sound.

- Use their fingers to form the letter that shows the sound-symbol relationship. This will work with letters such as *C, I, L, T,* and *O.*

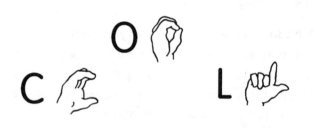

- Hold up a card with the letter or letters that show the sound-symbol relationship.

- Write the letter(s) that show the sound-symbol relationship on a sheet of paper each time they hear the sound. After you read the poem, ask children to count the number of times they wrote the letter(s). Then tell them how many times the sound actually occurs in the poem.

Using the Words in the Poem Display the poem on chart paper or in a pocket chart. Give children a variety of opportunities to *say* the words with the targeted sound. Keep in mind that it is important for children to both listen to the sound and articulate the sound in order to learn it. The following activities can provide listening and speaking opportunities:

- **Say Each Word** Have children say each word with the targeted sound after you model it. Emphasize the sound in the word and ask children to emphasize it as well.

- **Create a Word Wall** Create a word wall for groups of words with the targeted sound-letter relationship(s). Have children work in pairs or small groups to read the words as part of their learning-center time. Then invite children to think of additional words for each targeted sound-letter relationship. Add these words to the word wall. Or have children draw or cut out pictures of objects and help them label the pictures.

- **Segment Sounds** If the targeted sound is an initial or final sound, have children segment the sound. For example, if the targeted sound is /j/*j*, have children use a word from the poem, such as *jog* or *jungle,* and segment the initial sound: 1) Ask the child to say the word *jog.* 2) Ask the child to say the word *jog* again, this time leaving off the initial /j/*j*. If you are working with a final sound, such as /g/*g*: 1) Ask the child to say the word *pig.* 2) Ask the child to say the word *pig* again, leaving off the final /g/*g*. If the targeted sound is a medial sound, such as short *a,* have children segment initial and final sounds to focus on the sound of short *a*: 1) Ask the child to say the word *can.* 2) Ask the child to say the word *can* again, this time leaving off the initial /c/*c*. 3) Ask the child to say the word *can* once more, this time leaving off the final /n/*n*.

- **Pantomime Words** Invite a child to choose one of the words from the poem with the targeted sound-letter relationship and pantomime it. The rest of the children try to figure out the word. Give several children a turn.

Poetry Activities

Each of the following activities can be used with all or most of the poems in the book:

- **Word Substitution** Ask children to substitute different words for words with the targeted sound-letter relationship in the poem. This activity works particularly well with poems that name objects or actions, or contain proper names with the targeted sound-letter relationship.

- **Write a Verse** Since most of the poems are written with very definite rhyme and rhythm patterns, invite children to write an additional verse for the poem. Ask that the verse contain at least one (or two or three) words with the targeted sound-letter relationship.

- **Make Up a Title** Ask children to make up a new title for the poem. Ask them to be sure that at least one word in the new title has the targeted sound-letter relationship. For those

children who want a challenge, ask for two words in the title with the targeted sound-letter relationship.

- **Write a Poem** Ask children to write their own poems that use the targeted sound-letter relationship. Have children work in pairs, if they prefer. Bind all the children's poems into your own classroom anthology. Call it "P is for Poetry."

- **Poetry Puppet** Create a "poetry puppet" for your classroom. Some children may want to use the poetry puppet to "help" them as they recite or compose poems. You may also want to create a special poetry corner.

- **Make a Mobile** Ask children to use words with the targeted sound-letter relationship from the poem to create a mobile. They may want to draw or cut out pictures for the words they choose, label them, and then hang them with yarn from their mobiles.

- **Draw or Paint a Picture** Since most of the poems were written to create a picture or a story, ask children to draw or paint a picture that depicts the poem. Children may also want to write a caption for their picture. As children share their pictures, have them tell which objects or characters have names with the targeted sound-letter relationship.

- **Write a Riddle** Have children write a riddle about one of the words in the poem with the targeted sound-letter relationship. Help them set up the pattern of the riddle in the following way: The first sentence of the riddle should name the targeted sound, for example: "I have the long *o* sound." The next two sentences should give clues: "I am something you wear." "I keep you warm." The riddle should end with the question, "What am I?" (*coat*) Children can exchange riddles with a partner.

- **Record a Poem** Tape-record the poem so that children may listen to it frequently in your listening or poetry center. Encourage children to learn the poem and to recite it with a partner or in a small group. You may then want to tape-record the children's readings of the poem.

- **Choral Reading** Invite children to do choral readings of the poem. You can divide the class into groups so that each group reads specific lines or stanzas, depending on the pattern of the poem.

- **Write a Sentence** Ask children to write one or two sentences that tell about the poem. Each sentence should include one word with the targeted sound-letter relationship.

- **Questions and Answers** Have each child write a question about the poem. The question should include at least one word with the targeted sound-letter relationship, for example, "What kind of dog did **L**ou get?" Children then exchange papers and answer each other's questions with complete sentences. Answers should also include at least one word with the targeted sound-letter relationship, for example, "**L**ou got a **L**abrador pup."

- **Simple Crossword Puzzles** Ask children to choose two or three words with the targeted sound-letter relationship from the poem. Have them connect the words to create simple crossword puzzles.

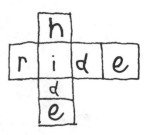

School-to-Home Letter

A letter such as the one below can be sent home along with any poem in the book. Be sure to include the letter or letters that stand for the sound-symbol relationship the poem supports. The letter and poem will give parents and caregivers the opportunity to participate in their children's phonics instruction, and will give children another chance to practice their phonics skills.

School-to-Home Letter

Dear _____,

Attached to this letter you will find a copy of a poem the children have been listening to in class. This poem helps children practice the sound that is made by the letter(s) _____.

It would be very helpful if you could take a few minutes to do one or more of the following activities with your child: 1) Read the poem several times to or with your child. Then ask your child to name some of the words that have the sound made by the letter(s) _____. 2) Help your child think of other familiar words that have the sound made by the letter(s) _____. 3) Ask your child to draw a picture that illustrates one of the words with the sound made by the letter(s) _____. Help your child write the word on the picture.

Thank you very much for your participation.

Sincerely,

_____

Bears on Bicycles

Balloons, **b**anjos, **b**ears on **b**icycles,

Baseball in the park.

Baskets, **b**aths, **b**umblebees, **b**irthdays,

Bedtime after dark.

Bananas, **b**oats, **b**uttons, **b**uses,

Birds that sing to me.

How many things can you think of

That **b**egin with the letter **b**?

Bear Dreams

When **b**ears go to sleep for winter,

They have a long, long time to dream.

Do you think they dream about **b**ears on **b**icycles

Or **b**ears that eat ice cream?

Do you think they dream about **b**ears in tall **b**uildings

Watching people walk far **b**elow?

Or do they dream about an all-**b**ear **b**aseball team

With one more inning to go?

Favorite Colors

What's your favorite color?

I asked my friend Colleen.

She said her favorite color

Is a deep forest green.

Can you tell me your favorite color?

I asked my friend Fred.

Fred said his favorite color

Is fire-engine red.

I asked my friend Carol

What color she liked most.

She said her favorite color

Is the color of toast.

Can you tell me your favorite color?

I asked my friend Sue.

She said her favorite color

Is a very dark blue.

I saw my friend Carl.

Carl is such a great fellow.

What's your favorite color, Carl?

He said it was bright yellow.

Now if you were to ask

The same question of me,

I'd say my favorite color

Is the color of the sea.

I Like **D**ogs!

Do you like **d**ogs?
I **d**o! I **d**o!
I like **d**achshunds
And **D**almatians too.

I like Great **D**anes
With their **d**eep, lou**d** bark,
If I ha**d** a **d**og,
We woul**d** walk in the park.

Mom and **D**ad, **d**on't forget
My birthday's coming up,
So I hope you **d**ecide
I **d**eserve to have a pup!

Another **D**ay

Tomorrow is another **d**ay

To **d**o the things that I must **d**o.

I **d**on't have any time today,

Tomorrow is another **d**ay.

Then I'll clean my room, I say,

Then I'll wee**d** the garden too.

Tomorrow is another **d**ay

To **d**o the things that I must **d**o.

Tomorrow has become today:

My **d**a**d** just hande**d** me a broom.

Da**d** says I can go out and play

As soon as I clean up my room!

A **F**awn in the **F**orest

While walking in the **f**orest,

I saw **f**ootprints in the snow,

And I **f**ollowed those **f**ootprints

To see where they would go.

I walked **f**or a while, and what did I see?

A sweet little **f**awn was staring at me.

"Hello, little **f**awn," I started to say.

But that **f**air little **f**awn ran quickly away.

Four Seasons

Some **f**olks like the winter
When the weather is cold.
Some **f**olks like the **f**all
When the colors are bold.

Some **f**olks like the spring
When **f**ields of flowers grow.
Some **f**olks like the summer
When they can swim and row.

But i**f** you want to know
My **f**avorite season of all,
I'd have to say without delay
My **f**avorite season is **f**all!

Gabby and **G**unther

Gabby the **g**oat and her brother **G**unther
Live with Farmer **G**il.
Each afternoon **G**abby and **G**unther
Play **g**ames at the top of the hill.

One day they played a **g**uessing **g**ame.
Gunther said, "Can you **g**uess who I am?
Baa, baa, baa, baa."
"I know," **G**abby said, "you're a lamb!"

Then it was **G**abby's turn to pretend.
She said, "Can you **g**uess who I am?"
She curled herself up and said nothing at all.
"I know," **G**unther said, "you're a clam!"

A **G**oldfish for **G**ilda

Today is **G**ilda's birthday.

Uncle **G**us **g**ave her a surprise.

When **G**ilda saw just what she **g**ot,

She couldn't believe her eyes.

Uncle **G**us **g**ave **G**ilda a pet

That was the answer to her wish.

It wasn't a turtle or a **g**uinea pi**g**,

It was simply a **g**orgeous **g**oldfish!

Hurray for **H**olidays

Hurray, **h**urray, it's a **h**oliday!

I can sleep late and it's okay.

I can play at **h**ome or ride my bike,

My friends and I can take a **h**ike.

We can **h**ave fun playing **h**ide-and-seek.

There's no **h**urry—it's a **h**oliday week!

Harry's Hamster Hal

Harry bought himself a hamster,

He named his hamster Hal.

But Hal was more than just a hamster,

He was almost like a pal.

As soon as Harry got home from school,

He'd tell Hal about his day.

Hal would sit and carefully listen

To each word that Harry would say.

At night when Harry shut the light,

He said, "Sleep tight!" to Hal.

Hal winked and blinked as if to say,

"I'm happy you're my pal!"

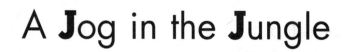

A **J**og in the **J**ungle

One day as I **j**ogged in the **j**ungle,

I saw a **j**aguar in a tree.

"Hello, **J**ogger," said the **j**aguar,

"Will you be friends with me?"

"Why certainly, Mr. **J**aguar," I said,

"Come **j**oin me as I run.

We can **j**ump and play and **j**og all day

Beneath the **j**ungle sun!"

Join In

All the kids who live on our block
Like to do different things.
John and Julie like to draw,
Jessica dances and sings.

Josh and Jane do jigsaw puzzles,
Justin likes to hike,
Jackie tells such funny jokes,
Jonathan likes to bike.

Come and join our happy block,
And do what you like to do.
Whether you jog or like to skate,
We would welcome you!

Sick Day

Kate got sick on Saturday
With fever and a cold.
Now Kate has to stay in bed
And do as she is told.

Outside, the kids are having fun,
They run and kick the ball.
Poor Kate is stuck inside all day.
That's hardly fair at all!

Everyone is kind to Kate.
Her dad shows her a trick,
Mom gives her lots of chicken soup,
The cat gives her a lick!

Her brother Rick says, "Don't be sad,
There are lots of things to do,
And look, Kate, now it's raining!
So your friends are inside too!"

Lou and Lee

Lou got a Labrador pup one day,
She named her Labrador Lee.
The moment Dad came home with him,
Lou said, "That dog's for me!"

Lee followed Lou wherever she went,
They were never far apart.
Lee was a sweet and gentle dog
With a large and loving heart.

As time went by, Lee grew and grew,
No longer a cute little pup,
But Lou didn't mind that Lee was large.
She said, "We're both growing up!"

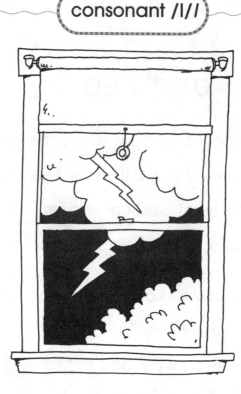

Thunder and Lightning

Late one night as I lay in bed,

I heard a loud noise overhead.

I ran to the window to see what was up

And was joined very quickly by Lucky, my pup.

We saw lightning flash through the sky,

A zigzag of light went blazing by.

"Don't be frightened by lightning," I said

As Lucky and I leaped back in bed!

Lucky sat on my lap, and I held him tight

Until we finally saw the last flashes of light.

That's when scared little Lucky heard me say,

"The storm is over and we're okay!"

Manny Is Moving

Manny felt sad and a little bit mad
When the moving truck came that day.
He was leaving behind so many good friends,
His family was moving away.

Manny was brave and tried not to cry
As he moved to his brand new home.
He missed good friends like Michael and Kim,
He was feeling so very alone.

Then one day, as he walked to school,
He met Maria and Mark,
And after school, he met Matthew,
And they rode their bikes to the park.

Now Manny is very happy once more,
He's made so many new friends.
Maybe moving wasn't so bad after all,
And this is how Manny's story ends!

My Favorite Month

My favorite month of the year is March,
I bet you don't know why.
Well then, let me tell you,
I'm not the type who's shy!

March is the month of my birthday,
And I know from my mom this is right.
I was born on Monday, the first of March,
In the middle of the night!

Names That Begin With N

How many **n**ames ca**n** you think of
That begi**n** with the letter **N**?
I ca**n** think of **n**ine **n**ames
And maybe eve**n** te**n**!

There's **N**at, **N**eal, **N**icholas,
Norman and **N**oll,
Nan, **N**ell, and **N**atalie,
Nisha, and **N**icole.

I came up with te**n** **n**ames,
So **n**ow I've done my part.
Ca**n** you **n**ame te**n** others?
Go ahead and start!

...Nat, Neal, Nicholas, Norman, Noll, Nan, Nell, Natalie, Nisha, Nicole...

Favorite **N**umber

What's your favorite **n**umber?
My favorite **n**umber's **n**ine.
That's because I'm **n**ine years old,
So I think of **n**ine as mine.

Next year my favorite **n**umber
Will probably be te**n**.
It'll be my favorite for a year
And the**n** **n**ot ever agai**n**.

I guess you understand **n**ow,
My favorite will always be
The **n**umber that tells how old I am,
It's fu**n** that way, you see!

Paint a Poem

Poems are **p**ictures you **p**aint with your words,

You don't need **p**aints of yellow or green.

All you need is a **p**aper and **p**encil

And the words to describe what you've seen.

You can write about **p**urple **p**arachutes,

You can write about blossoms of **p**ink,

You can describe what a **p**ineapple tastes like,

You can say just what you think!

Poems are **p**ictures you **p**aint with your words,

It's my favorite thing to do.

All you need is a **p**aper and **p**encil,

Won't you try to **p**aint a **p**oem too?

Piggy Bank

Pop gave me a cute little **p**iggy bank.

He's **p**ainted a shade of **p**ale **p**ink.

When I **p**ut all my **p**ennies in **P**iggy,

He gives me a smile and a wink!

New Pups

Our dog **P**earl had six cute **p**ups,

They're as cute as **p**ups can be.

My sister and I decided

That their names should begin with **P**.

So this is what we named them:

Pokey, **P**epper, and **P**at,

Peanut, **P**owder, and **P**atches.

Now what do you think of that?

Quack, **Qu**ack

I was sitting under a tree,

Quietly reading my book,

When I suddenly heard loud **qu**acking sounds

And decided to take a look.

I saw ducks lined up in the water,

They seemed to be having a race,

So I figured I'd **qu**ietly watch them

To see who would take first place.

The ducks swam **qu**ickly across the lake

To reach the other side,

And much to my amazement,

The winner **qu**acked and bowed with pride.

One of the ducks gave the winner

A gold medal for first prize.

It was **qu**ite a sight to see,

I couldn't believe my eyes!

Rex and Rory

Rex Raccoon and his brother Rory

Ran to the library to hear a story.

Rex said to Rory, "I would like to hear

A story about a panda bear."

Rory said to Rex, "Wouldn't it be good

To hear about Little Red Riding Hood?"

Then Rex Raccoon and his brother Rory

Joined the circle to hear the story.

Mrs. Rabbit said, "Children, get ready to hear

A story about a funny reindeer."

Rex and Rory replied, "Oh that's okay!

We're ready to hear any story today!"

Sandals

One **s**ummer I got **s**andals,
They were my very first pair.
My other shoes laced in my feet,
But **s**andals left them bare.

When I wore my special **s**andals,
I felt **s**o happy and free.
I showed them off to **S**arah and **S**am,
I wanted my friends to **s**ee.

How I loved that pair of **s**andals!
I wouldn't put them away
Till autumn's chill nipped at my toes
One cool **S**eptember day.

Summer

Walking on the beach,

My toes **s**inking in the **s**and,

I look out at the **s**ea,

I look back at the land.

I look up at the **s**un

As it **s**et**s** in the sky.

Isn't **s**ummer wonderful?

Please time, don't fly by!

Time for Bed

Tick, tock,

It's time for bed,

But I'm not ready to go.

I want to talk,

I want to eat,

But Mom and Dad say, "No!"

So I give in,

I say, "Okay,"

I snuggle with my pup,

I shut my eyes,

I count ten sheep,

And soon the sun is up!

Words That Start with T

Tadpoles, **t**ulips, **t**ambourines,

Tall **t**ales, **t**igers, **t**oo,

Teachers, **t**eamwork, **t**ents, and **t**ubas,

Tomatoes for me and for you.

Tacos, **t**urtles, **t**elephones,

Toys for you and for me.

Can you think of any other words

Tha**t** begin with the letter **t**?

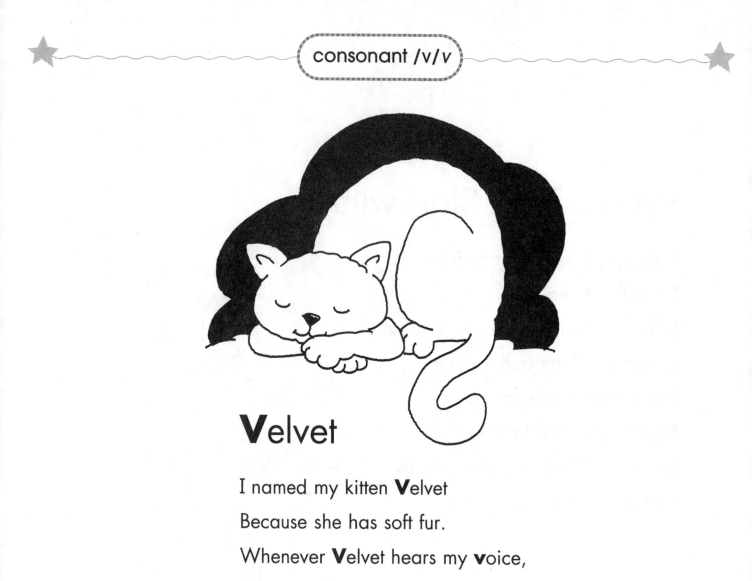

Velvet

I named my kitten **V**elvet
Because she has soft fur.
Whenever **V**elvet hears my **v**oice,
She starts to purr and purr.

One day I took sweet **V**elvet
For a **v**isit to the **v**et.
Dr. **V**ega smiled and said,
"What a **v**ery wonderful pet!"

I think if a contest were held
To choose the **v**ery best cat,
I'd have to **v**ote for **V**elvet,
There'd be no doubt of that!

Winter **W**eather

Most people like **w**arm **w**eather,

Or so I have been told,

But me, I like the **w**inter,

When the **w**eather is brisk and cold.

Each year I **w**ait for **w**inter,

With its **w**ind and snow and sleet.

I like to **w**ear my **w**arm **w**ool clothes

And boots upon my feet.

In **w**inter I go sledding

And skating in the park.

The **w**ind may blow and it may snow,

But I **w**on't come home till dark!

Max Can Relax

Max the fox worked very hard,
He worked the whole day through.
He never stopped to play or relax,
There was always too much to do!

On Mondays, Max would wax the floor,
On Tuesdays, Max would bake,
On Wednesdays, Max would fix his clothes,
On Thursdays, Max would rake.

One Friday, six of Max's pals
Came by and said to him,
"Max, you must mix work with play,
So let's go for a swim!"

Max and his pals went for a swim
Down by the shady creek.
Max had fun and asked his friends,
"Can we do this every week?"

My Friend **Y**olanda

I was playing in my **y**ard
When I saw a girl pass by.
She had just moved in next door,
And I stopped and **y**elled out, "Hi!"

"How are **y**ou!" she called to me,
"I just moved in **y**esterday.
My name is **Y**olanda.
Wouldn't it be fun to play?"

"**Y**es, it would!" I said to her,
"**Y**asmin is my name.
You and I can play all day,
I will show **y**ou my new game!"

Zelda and Zoe

Zelda the zebra lives in the zoo.

Zelda's cousin Zoe lives there too.

Zelda and Zoe always have lunch

With their favorite zookeeper, Zack.

The zebras carry some games to play,

And Zack brings their lunch in his pack.

Cecil and George

Cecil and **G**eorge were two **g**iraffes
Who de**c**ided to run a ra**c**e.
Cecil was lar**g**er with legs that were longer,
But **G**eorge had a steadier pace.

All their friends were very ex**c**ited
To watch **C**ecil and **G**eorge run the ra**c**e.
Everyone crowded around the track,
It was hard to find a good pla**c**e.

Cecil and **G**eorge ran the track twi**c**e,
They were very close indeed.
Cecil was running as fast as he could,
And **G**eorge was ra**c**ing with speed.

When it was over, the ra**c**e was a tie,
And both **G**eorge and **C**ecil had won.
Now they ra**c**e at least on**c**e a week
Because running and ra**c**ing are fun!

Sam's Pet

Sam asked his mom,
"Can I have a pet?"
Mom said to Sam,
"You're not old enough yet."

Sam asked his mom,
"How about a little lamb?"
Mom smiled and said,
"No lamb for us, dear Sam!"

Sam asked his mom,
"Can I have a giraffe?"
Mom smiled and said,
"Sam, you make me laugh!"

Sam said to Mom,
"A jaguar would be good."
Mom smiled and said,
"I don't think we should!"

Sam asked his mom,
"How about a toucan?"
Mom smiled and said,
"That isn't a good plan!"

At last, Sam asked his mom,
"What about a cat?"
Mom smiled and said,
"Okay, we can live with that!"

Funny **E**lephants

Have you **e**ver seen an **e**lephant
Ring a b**e**ll outside a school?
No, I've only seen an **e**lephant
Eating ch**e**stnuts by the pool!

Have you **e**ver seen an **e**lephant
In the c**e**nter of a lake?
No, I've only seen an **e**lephant
H**e**lp hims**e**lf to birthday cake!

Have you **e**ver seen an **e**lephant
Sitting in a d**e**ntist's chair?
No, I've only seen an **e**lephant
Napping with a t**e**ddy bear!

Have you **e**ver seen an **e**lephant
Eating scrambled **e**ggs and ham?
No, I've only seen an **e**lephant
Eating toast and ch**e**rry jam!

Have you **e**ver seen an **e**lephant
Write a l**e**tter with a p**e**n?
No, I've only seen an **e**lephant
Watching TV in the d**e**n!

Have you **e**ver seen an **e**lephant
Flying in an airplane?
No, I've only seen an **e**lephant
S**e**ll umbr**e**llas in the rain!

Have you **e**ver seen an **e**lephant
T**e**ll a story to a cat?
No, I've only seen an **e**lephant
Wear a bright r**e**d coat and hat!

Now I think it's time for me to **e**nd
This silly **e**lephant rhyme,
Unl**e**ss you'd like to add a verse—
You'll have a v**e**ry good time!

Invisible

If I could be **in**visible,

I'd take a l**i**ttle walk.

I'd stand right next to people,

And l**i**sten to them talk.

I'd go to the movies,

And I'd watch at least four.

It would not be d**i**fficult

To sl**i**p **i**n through the door!

If I Could Have a Party

If I could have a party
And invite anyone I like,
I'd ask a penguin and a grizzly bear
And a gorilla on a bike!

If I could have a party
And invite anyone at all,
I'd ask a chipmunk and a chimpanzee
And an ostrich six feet tall!

If I could have a party
And invite anyone I choose,
I'd ask an iguana and a silver fox
And the hippos in the zoos!

A Jog in the Fog

Tick tock, it's four o'clock,
It's time to go and jog.
Ron, John, Connie, and Bonnie
Run out into the fog.

"I cannot see!" Ron exclaims,
"The fog's so thick and gray.
Maybe we should go inside
And jog another day."

"Ron is right," Bonnie agrees,
"Come to my house and play.
Follow me, we're almost there,
It's just a block away."

Opposites

Do you know about **o**pposites?
Let's see if you do!
What's the **o**pposite of *many*?
The **o**pposite is *few*.

What's the **o**pposite of *b**o**ttom*?
The **o**pposite is *t**o**p*.
And what's the **o**pposite of *go*?
The **o**pposite is *st**o**p*.

What's the **o**pposite of *cold*?
The **o**pposite is *h**o**t*.
And what's the **o**pposite of *a little*?
The **o**pposite is *a l**o**t*.

Here is the last pair of **o**pposites.
Get ready, it's going to be hard!
What's the **o**pposite of *even*?
The **o**pposite is **o**dd.

HOW TALL ARE YOU?

Under the Cat's Umbrella

"Come under my umbrella,"
Cat said as Duck ran by.
"It's raining very hard now,
And I can keep you dry."

Duck ran under Cat's umbrella
And said, "Thank you, friendly Cat.
It's raining very hard now,
And I didn't bring my hat!"

"Come under my umbrella,"
Cat said as Pup ran by.
"It's raining very hard now,
And I can keep you dry."

Pup ran under Cat's umbrella
And said, "How kind of you.
It's coming down like cats and dogs,
And I'm soaked through and through!"

The three were under Cat's umbrella
When they saw a little bug.
"Come under the umbrella!" they called.
"It's nice and dry and snug."

Bug ran under Cat's umbrella
And said, "You're very kind to me.
The puddles are so deep now,
It's like swimming in the sea!"

The four were under Cat's umbrella
When Cat yelled, "There's the sun!
No need for the umbrella now,
It's time to have some fun!"

Flying On a Plane

I took my first trip on a pl**a**n**e**
To pay a visit to Aunt J**a**n**e**.
I went alone, I was very br**a**v**e**.
Mom told me that I must beh**a**v**e**.

A flight attendant, whose n**a**m**e** was Gr**a**c**e**,
Helped me with my blue suitc**a**s**e**.
The pl**a**n**e** took off, right on time,
And soon the pl**a**n**e** began to climb!

Everything below f**a**d**e**d from view,
The trees, the l**a**k**e**s, the rooftops too.
I g**a**v**e** a w**a**v**e**, as if to say,
"Good-by land, I'm flying away!"

I sat beside a man n**a**m**e**d W**a**d**e**
Who talked about machines he m**a**d**e**.
Gr**a**c**e** g**a**v**e** us lots of snacks to eat.
Food on a pl**a**n**e** was quite a treat!

After we **a**t**e**, as I g**a**z**e**d at the sky,
I knew I really liked to fly.
The pl**a**n**e** landed much too soon,
I could have flown all afternoon!

What Do You Like to Do?

What kinds of things do you **like** to do?

Do you **like** to r**ide** a b**ike**,

Skate on **ice**, or go for a h**ike**?

That's what I **like** to do!

What other things do you **like** to do?

Do you **like** to d**ive** in a pool,

Fly a k**ite**, or go to school?

That's what I **like** to do!

What else do you **like** to do?

Do you **like** to race to the finish l**ine**,

Eat **ice** cream, or stay up past n**ine**?

That's what I **like** to do!

What other things do you **like** to do?

Do you **like** to watch the t**ide**,

Run and h**ide**, or come down a sl**ide**?

That's what I **like** to do!

What else do you **like** to do?

Do you **like** to watch the sun r**ise**,

Eat French fries, or win a pr**ize**?

That's what I **like** to do!

What kinds of things do you **like** to do?

You can wr**ite** your own rhyme,

And have a good **time**,

And share all the things that you **like** to do!

My Friend Rose

My friend Rose moved far away.
I'm feeling quite alone.
Mom said, "Don't pout or mope about,
Just call her on the phone."

So I called Rose and we spoke awhile.
Now I feel a whole lot better.
And this morning after I woke up,
I wrote my friend a letter!

North P**o**le Dream

I was riding on a train
When my eyes began to cl**o**se,
And before I even knew it,
I began to dream and d**o**ze.

In my dream, I dr**o**ve a car
Up to the cold North P**o**le
Where I very nearly fr**o**ze
When I took a morning stroll.

I was glad when I w**o**ke up,
That I really didn't go
Up to the cold North P**o**le,
With its blanket of white snow.

June Can Sing

My dog **Ju**ne is very **cu**te,
Although she's quite h**uge**, too,
And every time I play my fl**ute**,
June knows just what to do.

June howls as I play my fl**ute**,
She thinks she's singing a song,
And as I continue to play my t**une**,
June keeps on singing along!

Duke the Mule

I have a m**ule**, his name is D**uke**,

And sometimes he is r**ude**,

But it's only when D**uke** is hungry

That he gets in a very bad mood.

When D**uke** is hungry, he won't move.

That's no exc**use**, I know,

But then if I give him an apple,

D**uke** will follow wherever I go!

Tod**ay** Is My Birthd**ay**

Tod**ay** will be a wonderful d**ay**,

Tod**ay** I will be eight!

I'll have a birthd**ay** party,

And I can hardly w**ai**t.

My friends and I will pl**ay** some games,

And then we'll get to eat.

After that I m**ay** open my presents,

Tod**ay** just can't be beat!

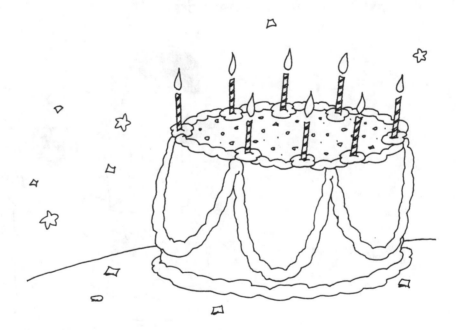

W**ai**ting for the M**ai**l

Every d**ay** without f**ai**l
I w**ai**t for the m**ai**l.
In r**ai**n and snow and h**ai**l,
I w**ai**t for the m**ai**l!

I w**ai**t for a letter from my pen pal, J**ay**,
Who lives in a country that is far aw**ay**.
Finally, on Frid**ay**, his letter comes my w**ay**,
And I write J**ay** back the very next d**ay**!

Sweet Dreams

One night Neal went to sleep
And had a very happy dream.
He dreamed he ate three bowls
Of chocolate-chip ice cream.

The very next morning,
When Neal was wide awake,
He said, "Next time I dream,
I'd like to eat some cake!"

Picnic M**ea**l

Aunt Jenn**y** and I had a picnic

Ben**ea**th shad**y** tr**ee**s near a cr**ee**k.

W**e** had lots of good things to f**ea**st on,

W**e** had prepared our food for a w**ee**k!

W**e** brought chicken and salad and freshl**y** squ**ee**zed juice,

There were p**ea**ches and muffins to **ea**t,

And last, but not l**ea**st, w**e** had r**ea**lly great brownies—

What an incredible tr**ea**t!

The Lion and the Butterfly

One day in the jungle,
A lion was napping
When he suddenly felt
A very slight tapping.

On top of his head
A butterfly had landed.
"What are you doing?"
The lion demanded.

The butterfly got frightened
And started to cry.
"I didn't mean to disturb you!"
He said with a sigh.

"I'm sorry, dear lion,
To be such a pest,
But I was tired of flying,
And I needed to rest."

The big lion looked up
At the shy butterfly
And felt very bad
That he caused him to cry.

"It's okay, little butterfly,"
He said in reply.
"You can rest on my head
Until you're ready to fly."

Sn**ow**fall

Early this morning
I looked out my wind**ow**.
Everything was white,
It sn**ow**ed last night!

The streets were s**o** quiet,
The silence was t**o**tal,
There was n**o** place to g**o**
Because of the sn**ow**.

The schools were not **o**pen,
The r**oa**ds were not clear,
The sn**ow**drifts stood tall,
And sn**ow** continued to fall!

I put on my c**oa**t,
And hat, boots, and gloves,
To meet my friend J**oe**
To play in the sn**ow**.

We played for an hour,
Or perhaps it was two,
Then J**oe** said with a smile,
"Let's g**o** in for a while."

That was fine with me,
My t**oe**s were s**o** c**o**ld!
I said with a grin,
"You can foll**ow** me in!"

Holiday Sp**ar**ks

On July 4th weekend

My friend M**ar**k and I

Went to watch fireworks

At a p**ar**k nearby.

The sp**ar**ks exploded color

Against a sky so d**ar**k

Red, white, and blue

Lit up the whole p**ar**k!

A **Mar**velous St**ar**ry Sky

Last summer I camped in a p**ar**k
And slept outside each night
Beneath a **lar**ge and st**ar**ry sky
That was quite a m**ar**velous sight!

My favorite p**ar**t of the day
Was when I'd go to sleep.
I'd try to count each sp**ar**kling st**ar**
Instead of counting sheep!

I Wonder

Do you ever wonder
What you'll grow up to be?
A nurse or a doctor,
Perhaps you'll sail the sea!

You might be a painter
Or turn out to be a vet,
Treating birds and turtles,
And every kind of pet!

You could be an astronomer
Who studies all the stars,
A teacher, or an astronaut,
The first to land on Mars!

A Horse Named Cora

I have a horse named Cora.
She lives on a farm with me.
Cora is no ordinary horse,
She's as special as a horse can be.

When I feed Cora each morning,
We talk, and talk some more,
Then I'm off to school for the day,
And I don't return till four.

After I get home from school,
And all my chores are done,
I take Cora out for a ride.
There's nothing that's more fun!

Little B**ear**

"Come inside my cozy house,"
I said to Little B**ear**.
"It's nice and warm inside my house,
And the weather's bad out th**ere**."

Little B**ear** came in my house.
His h**air** was icy and wet.
"How kind of you," he said to me,
"Since I know we've never met."

"You're welcome, Little B**ear**," I said.
"Here's a towel for your h**air**.
Now take a seat and rest your feet
While I prep**are** a meal to sh**are**!"

A D**eer** Family

While playing in my yard one day,
I suddenly did h**ear**
The sound of rustling noises,
And saw a family of d**eer**.

The d**eer** were walking in the woods
Right h**ere**, behind my house!
And I could sit n**ear**by and watch,
As quiet as a mouse!

I watched the d**eer** for a little while,
The baby, the mom, and the dad,
But all too soon they disapp**ear**ed.
What a special time I had!

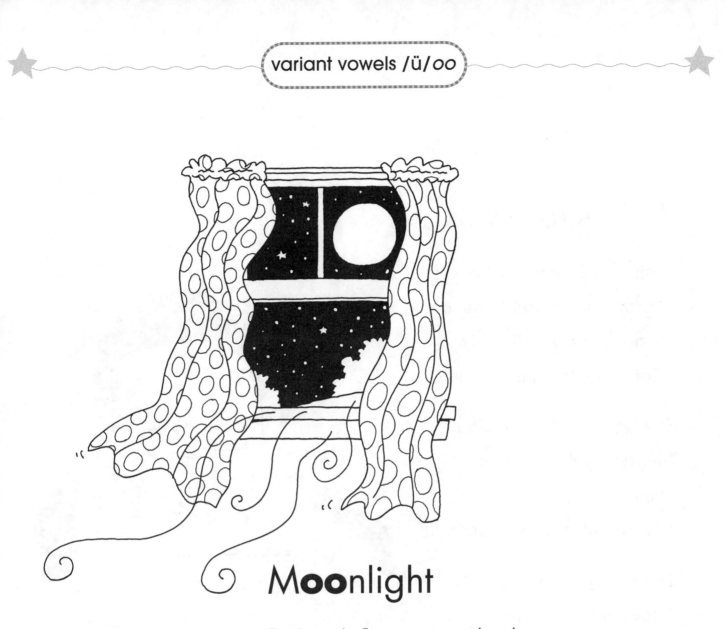

Moonlight

Each night I gaze up at the sky.

I like to watch the m**oo**n.

Sometimes it's just a crescent slice,

Sometimes a round ball**oo**n.

In my r**oo**m I see the m**oo**n

And open the window wide.

I want the m**oo**nlight from above

To make its way inside.

A Good Book

Yesterday I read a book
That was too good to put down,
Even when my dad said,
"Come on, let's bike to town!"

The book was so exciting
I hardly looked up at all,
Even when my friends said,
"Come out and play football!"

I kept on reading the book,
It took the entire day,
And when I was finally done,
I felt like I'd been far away!

My Bl**ue** Balloon

I was holding my big bl**ue** balloon
When a strong gust of wind bl**ew** by,
Then my big bl**ue** balloon bl**ew** away,
And I saw it float up to the sky!

I kn**ew** my balloon was gone
When it fl**ew** toward the clouds so high,
Then my big bl**ue** balloon did a dance in the air,
As if it were waving good-by!

Dr**aw**ing Pictures

I like to dr**aw a**ll kinds of things,

Pictures of astron**au**ts,

Dinos**au**rs, and kings,

Pictures of t**a**ll giraffes

Playing basketb**a**ll,

Pictures of mice

In their houses so sm**a**ll!

Pictures of **au**tumn

And children on swings,

I like to dr**aw a**ll kinds of things.

Merry-Go-Round

When I'm on a merry-go-round,

I get so very dizzy.

When I'm spinning round and round,

I find I'm in a tizzy.

But when my mom says,

"Let's get off now,"

I say, "Oh no, let's stay.

I want to go around one more time.

Please let me have my way!"

Lost and F**ou**nd

Mr. C**ow** was writing a shopping list
Of the things he had to buy
When, all of a sudden, he lost his pen,
And he sh**ou**ted, "Oh me! Oh my!"

Mr. C**ow** ran to see Mrs. **Ow**l,
Who was as wise as she could be.
He brought her a bunch of fl**ow**ers
And asked, "Mrs. **Ow**l, can you help me?"

"You see, I lost my pen before,
And I really don't know h**ow**,
But I have to write my shopping list,
And I have to do it n**ow**!"

Mrs. **Ow**l replied to Mr. C**ow**,
"I've f**ou**nd your pen, my dear.
You someh**ow** must have forgotten
That you put it behind your ear!"

J**oy**ce's Garden

Some people think J**oy**ce works too hard
Because she likes to t**oi**l
For hours and hours in her backyard,
With her hands deep in the s**oi**l.

J**oy**ce doesn't think she works too hard.
"It's not hard work, it's play!"
There's nothing J**oy**ce enj**oy**s as much
As planting flowers all day!

My Ch**oi**ce

I signed up for singing lessons.

I think I have a good v**oi**ce.

Mom didn't ask me to do it,

It was really my very own ch**oi**ce.

Whenever I sing, I feel j**oy**ous.

I rej**oi**ce with a tune or a song.

It makes me feel r**oy**al, like a princess or queen,

As if nothing could ever go wrong!

Spelling Te**st**

I had a **sp**elling te**st** today.

I hope that I did well,

But some of the words on my **sp**elling te**st**

Were very hard to **sp**ell!

I'll give you some examples

To show you what I mean:

Spaghetti, **sp**are, and **sp**arkle,

Skeleton, and *machine*!

Here are more examples;

These words are difficult too:

Skiing and **sk**yscraper,

Statue, **st**itch, and **st**ew!

Am I a very good **sp**eller?

Today I'm not too sure.

I'll let you know tomorrow

When I get my **sp**elling score!

Spri**ng**

Spri**ng** is my favorite season.

It bri**ng**s out the pla**nt**s and the flowers.

It's the very best time to sit on a swi**ng**

And daydream for hours and hours.

In summer I like to go swimmi**ng**.

In wi**nt**er I play in the snow.

In fall I enjoy all the colorful leaves,

But in spri**ng** I can watch flowers grow!

An Owl's So**ng**

Last night I spe**nt**

The whole night in a te**nt**,

Beneath the stars and the moon.

All the night lo**ng**

An owl sa**ng** its so**ng**.

What a wonderful cou**nt**ry tune!

Summer Ca**mp**

I went to summer ca**mp** this year

A**nd** had a wo**nd**erful time.

We'd fish in the po**nd** a**nd** swim and play,

We'd even hike a**nd** climb!

One day there was a ju**mp**ing race,

A**nd** I became the cha**mp**.

That might have been my favorite day

That I spent at summer ca**mp**!

Best Frie**nd**

A best frie**nd** is a special frie**nd**,
Someone on whom you can depe**nd**.
While best frie**nd**s aren't easily fou**nd**,
If you search, they're still arou**nd**.

A best frie**nd** should be ki**nd** to you
A**nd** like to have a good time too;
Someone who likes to ju**mp** a**nd** play,
A**nd** listens to the things you say.

A Special **Tr**ip

I took a **tr**ip the other day,

But I didn't take a **tr**ain,

I didn't **tr**avel by car or **tr**uck,

Or fly off in a plane.

I just sat under a shady **tr**ee,

And read my favorite book.

It took me to a place of **tr**easures—

The best **tr**ip I ever took!

The **Pr**ize

I **pr**acticed each day for the race.

I wanted to **pr**ove I could run.

I did my best to **pr**epare for the test,

And I even began to have fun!

When the day of the race arrived,

I was **pr**oud of my speed and my grace,

And to my sur**pr**ise, I took home the **pr**ize

For coming in second place!

Creatures Crawl and Creep

My friend **Cr**ystal and I
Walked down by the **cr**eek.
We heard the frogs **cr**oak,
We heard the **cr**ickets cheep.

We **pl**ayed quietly all day
And enjoyed each **pl**easant sound,
Watching nature's **cr**eatures **cr**awl and **cr**eep
Upon their own campground.

City **Pl**aces

We went to the city,
Uncle **Cr**aig and I.
It was the first time I saw
Buildings rise to the sky!

We went to museums
And other great **pl**aces,
And I was amazed
By the **cr**owds in small spaces.

We went to a **pl**ay,
Then we walked a**cr**oss the park
And had **pl**enty to eat
Before it got dark.

The one thing that **pl**eased me
Perhaps most of all
Was that people **cr**eated
Those buildings so tall!

Slippery Hill

On Saturday I took my **sl**ed

To the top of a **sl**ippery hill.

The **sn**ow was white, the day was bright,

And everything was still.

When I **sl**id down to the bottom,

I **sm**iled to myself, and then

I **sl**owly climbed that **sl**ippery hill

To **sl**ide back down again!

Snow Dream

Last night when I was fast a**sl**eep,

I dreamed it **sn**owed all night,

And everything around me

Looked soft and **sm**ooth and white.

When I woke up this morning,

I **sm**iled at a wonderful sight.

I didn't dream it after all,

It really **sn**owed last night!

Fly Away

Do you like to pretend
To **fl**y through the air,
High above **fl**uffy clouds,
Free **fr**om worry or care?

Do you like to pretend
To **fl**y off when you please,
To **fl**ap your arms quickly
And **fl**oat on a breeze?

Yes, I like to pretend
To **fl**y over a tree,
And sometimes I pretend
To **fl**y over the sea.

It's such fun to pretend
That I'm off on a **fl**ight,
Flying high, **fl**ying low,
In the dawn, in the night.

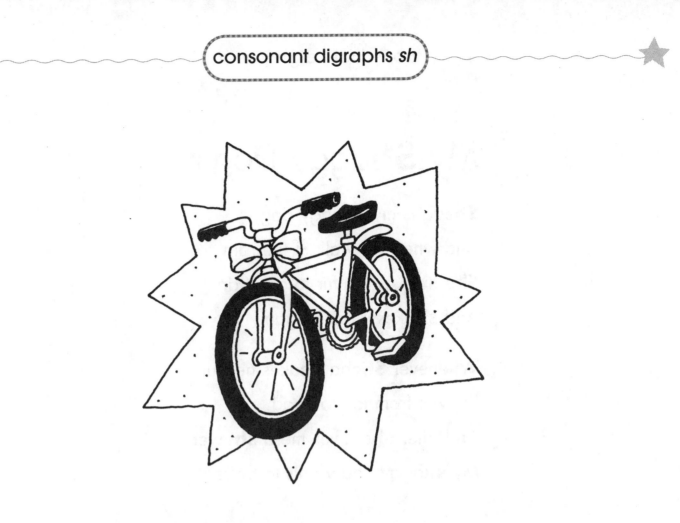

Wi**sh** Upon a Star

Last night I saw a **sh**ooting star
That danced across the sky.
I made a wi**sh** upon that star
As it went dancing by.

If Mom buys me a bike today
That's bright and **sh**iny and new,
I'll **sh**out so everyone will hear,
"Hooray, my wi**sh** came true!"

My **Sh**aggy Dog

Sheba is my **sh**aggy dog,
And when we walk in the rain,
She **sh**akes her fur to get it dry
And **sh**akes it once again!

Whenever **Sh**eba **sh**akes her fur,
I'm wet from toe to head,
And after **sh**e gives me a **sh**ower,
My **sh**aggy dog wants to be fed!

At **the** Ri**nk**

My bro**th**er took me skating
At an ice-skating ri**nk**.
There were people zooming past us
Quicker **th**an a bli**nk**!

I held my bro**th**er's hand
As we stepped out on **the** ice,
And I was ra**th**er **th**ankful
Just to skate around twice!

Letter to an Au**th**or

I read a book **th**e o**th**er day,

And I liked it quite a lot.

I **th**ought it was exciting,

Wi**th** a very mysterious plot.

So I wrote **th**e au**th**or a letter,

I'd never done **th**at before,

But I wanted to **th**a**nk** her for writing **th**e book,

And to ask her to write a few more!

At the Bea**ch**

Whenever I'm at the bea**ch**,
I get as hungry as can be.
I want to mun**ch** all day
As I play beside the sea.

Whenever I'm at the bea**ch**,
Dad brings a hearty lun**ch**.
We eat **ch**icken, **ch**eese, and pea**ch**es,
And **ch**erries by the bun**ch**!

After lun**ch** I build a castle
Or look at the sea and dream,
But soon I tou**ch** Dad's arm and ask,
"How about some **ch**ocolate ice cream?"

Chess With Gramp

I asked my grandpa,

"Will you tea**ch** me to play **ch**ess?"

Gramp said happily,

"Dear **ch**ild, the answer's, Yes!"

So ea**ch** Friday night

Gramp shows me something new,

And I play so mu**ch** better

By the time our lesson's through.

It's su**ch** a **ch**allenge

To play **ch**ess with my gramp,

But he thinks someday

I'll become a **ch**ess **ch**amp!

The **Wh**istling Wind

As I sat in a chair by the fireplace,

I heard the wind **wh**ispering low.

When I looked outside the window,

The leaves were beginning to blow.

Soon the **wh**isper turned into a **wh**istle

When the wind began **wh**istling its song.

Then I knew that a storm would be coming,

And it would be here before long.

White Snow

When I went for a walk today,

Whichever way I'd go,

All I could see were piles and piles

Of wonderful soft **wh**ite snow!

The clean **wh**ite snow was two feet deep,

For it had snowed a**wh**ile.

Some people didn't like it much,

But me—it made me smile!